RAIL ROVER
ANGLIA RANGER

Adam Head

AMBERLEY

Front Cover: DRS Class 37s Nos 37419 and 37422 power through Brandon with a light engine move to Crewe.

Rear Cover: On a semi-fast service for London Liverpool Street, Abellio Greater Anglia Class 90 No. 90008 accelerates past Stowmarket.

First published 2018

Amberley Publishing
The Hill, Stroud
Gloucestershire, GL5 4EP

www.amberley-books.com

Copyright © Adam Head, 2018

The right of Adam Head to be identified as the Author of this work has been asserted in accordance with the Copyrights, Designs and Patents Act 1988.

ISBN 978 1 4456 8167 2 (print)
ISBN 978 1 4456 8168 9 (ebook)

British Library Cataloguing in Publication Data. A catalogue record for this book is available from the British Library.

Origination by Amberley Publishing.
Printed in the UK.

Contents

Introduction

When thinking of places to go trainspotting, East Anglia is usually high on a lot of people's lists, but with the different places that make up the East Anglian rail network it can be hard to choose where to go initially.

That is where the Anglia Day Ranger ticket comes in; allowing unlimited train trips around Norfolk, Suffolk and Cambridgeshire, you will find that you are spoilt for choice as you decide which lines to traverse to take in the sights. The Anglia Day Ranger ticket allows travel down the following lines:

- The Bittern Line – Norwich to Sheringham
- The Breckland Line – Norwich to Cambridge
- The East Suffolk Line – Ipswich to Lowestoft and Felixstowe
- The Great Eastern Main Line – Norwich to London Liverpool Street*
- The Ipswich–Ely Line – Ipswich to Ely and Cambridge
- The Wherry Lines – Norwich to Great Yarmouth and Lowestoft

*An Anglia Day Ranger only allows you to travel as far as Ipswich.

An Anglia Day Ranger is valid seven days a week and can be bought as either one day or as a three in seven flexi rover, which allows you to travel any three days within a seven-day period, on Monday–Friday it can be bought and used after 08.45 and used until the end of service, and on weekends it can be bought and used at the start of service, remaining valid until the end of service.

The railways of East Anglia are made up of three operators, which are:

Abellio Greater Anglia

The main operator of East Anglia, they operate all the lines mentioned above on which an Anglia Day Ranger is valid. Their stock comprises a mix of loco-hauled and diesel and electric multiple units, and they run five Class 153 Sprinter DMUs, nine Class 156 Sprinter DMUs, twelve Class 170 Turbostar DMUs, fifteen Class 90s with British Rail Mk 3 carriages and Class 82 Driving Van Trailers (DVTs), fifty-eight Class 317 EMUs, 104 Class 321 EMUs, twenty-one Class 360 Desiro EMUs and thirty Class 379 Electrostar EMUs.

Norwich station, the main starting point for most journeys on an Anglia Day Ranger. From here, services to Cambridge, Great Yarmouth, London Liverpool Street, Lowestoft and Sheringham via Cromer can be boarded.

The Abellio Greater Anglia logo, as seen on a Class 170 Turbostar.

A 'Short Set' comprising two Class 37 diesel locomotives sandwiching two British Rail Mk 2 carriages also makes up part of Abellio Greater Anglia's stock.

At the time of writing, Abellio Greater Anglia have put in an order for 1,043 new carriages to replace their existing stock. This new stock will start coming into operation between 2019 and 2020.

East Midlands Trains

Operated by Stagecoach, East Midlands Trains run a service between Norwich and Liverpool Lime Street via Nottingham, Sheffield and Manchester and an Anglia Day Ranger allows you to travel on their services between Ely and Norwich. Their stock comprises seventeen Class 153 Sprinter DMUs, fifteen Class 156 Sprinter DMUs and twenty-six Class 158 Sprinter DMUs. They also have a fleet of twenty-four Class 43 HST power cars and twenty-seven Class 222 Meridian DEMUs, but they never run down to East Anglia.

The Class 158 Sprinter DMU is the primary unit that operates on the Norwich to Liverpool services, but sometimes they can be deputised with Class 156 Sprinter DMUs and on some occasions Class 153 Sprinter DMUs. This can be due to a number of reasons; for example, unit failure or unavailability.

The East Midlands Trains logo, as seen on a Class 158 Sprinter.

At the time of writing, the East Midlands franchise is currently up for renewal with either Stagecoach, the current operator, continuing to run the area or a new company taking over in 2019.

Great Northern

Great Northern, who make up part of the Govia Thameslink Railway franchise, run a service between King's Lynn and London King's Cross via Ely, Cambridge and the East Coast Main Line via Stevenage. An Anglia Day Ranger is valid on their services between Ely and Cambridge and allows unlimited travel between the two cities across the Cambridgeshire Fens. This operator's stock differs greatly to Abellio Greater Anglia and East Midlands Trains as theirs only consists of electric multiple units, with an Anglia Day Ranger train typically being made up of a mix of either forty Class 365 Networker EMUs or twenty-nine Class 387 Electrostar EMUs. Newer Class 700 Desiro EMUs are starting to make appearances at Cambridge in the hope of new services being created out of the city to other cities in the South.

The Great Northern logo, as seen on a Class 387 Electrostar.

The Arriva CrossCountry logo, as seen on a Class 170 Turbostar.

Between Cambridge and Ely there is a fourth operator called Arriva CrossCountry, who are the largest franchise in the UK, and they run a service from Birmingham New Street to Stansted Airport using a fleet of twenty-nine Class 170 Turbostar DMUs. Unfortunately, however, they do not allow Anglia Day Ranger tickets on their services.

The Bittern Line

A coastal line based out of Norwich that may be overshadowed by the Wherry Lines, the Bittern Line runs to Sheringham via Cromer. This is a 30-mile branch line and it was opened between 1874 and 1877. There are ten stations on the Bittern Line, which are as follows:

- Norwich
- Salhouse
- Hoveton & Wroxham
- Worstead
- North Walsham
- Gunton
- Roughton Road
- Cromer
- West Runton
- Sheringham

The line sees an hourly service, which is usually served by Class 153 and Class 156 Sprinters, although occasionally a two or three-carriage Class 170 Turbostar can be seen on this line despite the short platforms. The passenger numbers on this line have risen in recent years, meaning that Abellio Greater Anglia have started to increase passenger services on this line to allow for the extra numbers. Despite this, there is still room for a twice weekly freight train that runs to North Walsham with condensate tanks usually hauled by a GB Railfreight Class 66 diesel locomotive.

The Bittern Line has two preserved railways* nearby. First is the 9-mile narrow gauge Bure Valley Railway, which operates from Wroxham to Aylsham and which is usually connected to a Norfolk Broads cruise that allows travellers to explore the beauty and wonder of the Norfolk Broads from a tour boat. The Bure Valley Railway and the cruise boat tours work hand in hand and passengers can alight at Hoveton & Wroxham for the Bure Valley Railway. The second preserved railway is the North Norfolk Railway, which is a 5-mile standard gauge railway that runs from Sheringham to Holt. The railway was initially part of the former Midland & Great Northern Joint Railway (M&GN), which was built and run by William Marriott. The line was closed but in 1973 started to run again, with services being extended to Holt in 1989, and over the years this preserved railway has gone from strength to strength, with passenger numbers raising every year and many steam and diesel galas among other events attracting people. In 2010 a level crossing was built to allow the North Norfolk

Railway to be reconnected back to the national rail network and as a result trains can easily join and leave the railway without the need for road transport anymore. The railway provides many scenic views as it passes through the Norfolk countryside.

  *Additional tickets need to be bought for both the Bure Valley Railway and North Norfolk Railway.

Above: Abellio Greater Anglia Class 156 Sprinter No. 156417 sits at Norwich, awaiting departure for the Bittern Line with a service for Sheringham. These services do not sit in Norwich for very long, with the unit arriving at Norwich at XX.40 and then departing at XX.45.

Left: Four Class 156 Sprinters were branded by Abellio Greater Anglia, advertising the various lines that they run in East Anglia. Here, Class 156 Sprinter No. 156417 advertises the Bittern Line.

In some circumstances, passengers can travel on the Bittern Line in a three-carriage Turbostar, as seen here as Abellio Greater Anglia Class 170 Turbostar No. 170208 awaits departure at Norwich.

Abellio Greater Anglia Class 153 Sprinter No. 153314 sits at Norwich, awaiting departure with an early evening service for Sheringham.

Stations like Salhouse, seen here, receive a service once every two hours for both Norwich and Sheringham.

Class 153 Sprinter No. 153306 departs Salhouse for Norwich, where it will terminate.

An Abellio Greater Anglia Class 156 Sprinter makes its first stop at Salhouse on its way to Sheringham.

Abellio Greater Anglia Class 153 Sprinter No. 153309 sits at Hoveton & Wroxham with a very busy service for Norwich.

Abellio Greater Anglia Class 170 Turbostar No. 170207 arrives into Hoveton & Wroxham with a service for Sheringham.

Customers can alight at Hoveton & Wroxham for the Bure Valley Railway, a narrow-gauge railway which runs a total of 9 miles from Wroxham to Aylsham. Their fleet of trains has a few diesels but it mainly consists of steam engines, as seen in this image, which shows No. 6 *Blickling Hall* arriving into Wroxham on a sweltering hot day with a service from Aylsham.

The Bure Valley Railway has one narrow-gauge diesel train among its small fleet of steam engines. No. 3 *US Air Division USAAF* runs around at Wroxham before forming a train back to Aylsham.

North Walsham is one of the few double-track sections of the Bittern Line and is where services to Norwich and Sheringham meet. Here, Abellio Greater Anglia Class 153 Sprinter No. 153314 sits at North Walsham, awaiting departure for Norwich.

Abellio Greater Anglia Class 156 Sprinter No. 156422 arrives into North Walsham with a service for Norwich.

The picturesque station of Gunton, 19 miles away from Norwich, has been tastefully recreated to give passengers an idea of what the station would have looked like when it was owned by the Great Eastern Railway.

Gunton is like Salhouse, in so much that it is only served by trains every two hours, as seen here with Abellio Greater Anglia Class 153 Sprinter No. 153335 arriving with a service for Sheringham.

Cromer is an unusual station because for any services to get to and from Sheringham the driver must change ends here before carrying on. One such example is Class 170 Turbostar No. 170271, which is seen sitting at Cromer awaiting departure for Sheringham.

Abellio Greater Anglia Class 153 Sprinter No. 153306 sits at Cromer with a service for Sheringham.

At the end of the platform at Cromer station is Cromer Yard Signal Box, which is non-operational but can be visited by members of the public to get an insight into how a signal box like this would have worked on the Bittern Line.

Abellio Greater Anglia Class 153 Sprinter No. 153306 arrives into Cromer with a service for Norwich.

Despite services not meeting at Cromer, both platforms are used, with Platform 1 being used for services going to Sheringham and Platform 2 being used for services going to Norwich, as seen here with No. 156422.

Above and below: During the school holidays and summertime, the Bittern Line can get very busy. Therefore, capacity needs to be increased to accommodate the higher number of people. One example can be seen here with Abellio Greater Anglia Class 170 Turbostar No. 170207 being drafted onto Bittern Line services.

Between Cromer and Sheringham is the small station of West Runton, which sees an hourly service in each direction, as seen here with Nos 153314, 156422 and 153335.

The end of the line as Class 153 Sprinter No. 153309 sits at Sheringham, awaiting departure for Norwich. As you can see, Sheringham station is made up of a short platform, which can prove busy when the North Norfolk Railway is in operation.

Passengers can alight at Sheringham and walk over the road to the North Norfolk Railway. For a small fee, they can travel down the 10½-mile preserved railway to Holt. The NNR has a variety of different steam and diesel locomotives, with one such example being this stunning LNER B12, No. 8572, which regularly provides services up and down the line.

The North Norfolk Railway has also played host to many visiting diesel locomotives, with one being this Class 20 diesel locomotive, No. 20227, which was painted in London Underground colours for its 150th anniversary. In 2016, it visited the North Norfolk Railway for its yearly diesel gala.

The Breckland Line

A main route and the second busiest out of Norwich after the Great Eastern Main Line, the Breckland Line has run from Norwich to Cambridge since the Strategic Rail Authority set up the route between these two stations in 2002. This route has more to it than just serving the two cities of Norwich and Cambridge, however, as it also provides connections for the Midlands and the North from Ely.

The line, which was opened in 1845, is 68 miles long and is made up of thirteen stations, which are as follows:

- Norwich
- Wymondham
- Spooner Row*
- Attleborough
- Eccles Road
- Harling Road
- Thetford
- Brandon
- Lakenheath*
- Shippea Hill*
- Ely
- Cambridge North
- Cambridge

*Request stop only, please check timetable before trying to alight at one of these stations.

These hourly services are run by Class 170 Turbostar DMUs but sometimes a Class 156 Sprinter DMU or in some extreme cases a Class 153 Sprinter DMU can be found running these services, covering for the Turbostar to avoid the diagram being cancelled. When the Great Eastern Main Line is closed for planned engineering works on some weekends, this line then becomes the only main route into London and is favoured by commuters as they can then change at Cambridge North or Cambridge for a service to London Liverpool Street or London King's Cross.

There is a mix of both passenger and freight services on the Breckland Line. DB Cargo provides aggregate traffic to places such as Norwich, Eccles Road and now Brandon, with a new freight service having been opened here as of late 2017 from places such as Mountsorrel in Leicestershire and the Peak Forest in Derbyshire. Freightliner also provide aggregate traffic to Norwich from Tunstead in Derbyshire. Both of these operators use Class 66 diesel locomotives on their freight diagrams with their paint schemes being their main difference, with DB's bright red contrasting with the dark green of Freightliner.

In 2012 this line went through a major signalling upgrade, which meant that all the signal boxes were decommissioned, and all the semaphore signals were torn down and disposed of in favour of new colour aspect signals that were controlled and supervised by Cambridge Power Signal Box (PSB). This took away the nostalgic feeling that is still felt on lines such as the Wherry Lines (*Chapter 6*).

Unlike the other lines on an Anglia Day Ranger, this one has more than one operator running on it. East Midlands Trains also provides a service from Norwich to Liverpool, which on an ADR can allow you to go as far as Ely. This differs from Abellio Greater Anglia's service as, while theirs stops at Wymondham, Attleborough and Brandon, East Midlands Trains services are non-stop from Norwich to Thetford and then non-stop to Ely. Therefore, if a faster ride through the Norfolk countryside and the Cambridgeshire Fens is favoured then East Midlands Trains is your best bet; otherwise, Abellio Greater Anglia provides just as brilliant a service. From Ely – a medium sized station which is favoured by many train enthusiasts for the frequency of trains through the station (both passenger and freight) – two more operators appear in the form of Great Northern and Arriva CrossCountry, providing services for Cambridge, London King's Cross and Stansted Airport.

This line is still expanding, with a new station called Cambridge North opening in May 2017 for the surrounding areas of Cambridge. Previously, these areas could only be reached by bus from the city centre. This station is served by Abellio Greater Anglia and Great Northern and has become very popular with commuters, providing services for Norwich, Cambridge and London's King's Cross and Liverpool Street.

Cambridge differs greatly from Norwich, as Norwich station is occupied by DMUs and no EMUs, whereas at Cambridge the opposite is true.

Abellio Greater Anglia Class 170 Turbostar No. 170204 sits at Norwich, awaiting departure for Cambridge. When this picture was taken the cab and carriage had recently been rebuilt after it had been involved in an accident involving a tractor between Harling Road and Thetford. After hitting it at over 80 mph there was significant damage, which resulted in the whole unit being transported by road to Kilmarnock, Scotland, for repair.

Sometimes, when East Midlands Trains are unable to supply a Class 158 Sprinter for their Liverpool Lime Street services, a Class 156 Sprinter will step in instead, as seen here as Class 156 Sprinter No. 156406 awaits departure for Liverpool Lime Street.

Abellio Greater Anglia Class 170 Turbostar No. 170201 departs Norwich with an early morning service for Cambridge.

Not all freight trains that travel across the Breckland Line are aggregate trains; sometimes, engineer's trains, usually operated by GB Railfreight, will use the line to get to stations on the Bittern or Wherry Lines. When this picture of GB Railfreight Class 66 No. 66769 was taken at Wymondham, bound for Brundall Gardens, the Wherry Lines were closed for engineering works. Usually these engineer's trains will run very late at night or early in the morning so as not to disrupt passenger services.

The Mid Norfolk Railway, which runs from Dereham to Wymondham, hosts regular railway galas throughout the year. The convoy of trains going to the preserved railway will run to Wymondham, where it will be reversed and head towards Dereham. In April 2016, the Mid Norfolk Railway acquired three Class 50 diesel locomotives and the prototype HST for their Spring Diesel Gala, along with a few other diesel locos. Here, the convoy led by Class 50 D407 (No. 50007) is pulling into Wymondham station in preparation to reverse onto the Mid Norfolk.

Test trains are common all over the country and East Anglia also sees its fair share of them as they work their way around the main lines and branch lines. The photograph is a rarity because of the loco leading the test train, Class 37 No. 37025, which is heading through Wymondham, bound for Ely after reversing at Norwich.

The very scenic station at Wymondham sees a regular hourly service to both Norwich and Cambridge, as seen here with Abellio Greater Anglia Class 170 Turbostar No. 170201 awaiting departure for Cambridge. If you are unfortunate enough to miss the train, there is a very nice restaurant on the Norwich-bound platform to grab some food or a drink.

Alighting at Wymondham, a short walk away from the station is the pleasant Mid Norfolk Railway, which is a 15-mile journey through the Norfolk countryside from Wymondham to Dereham. Passengers can travel on trains such as the Class 101 DMU (No. 101695) seen in this image, which is awaiting departure for Dereham. These used to be a regular sight at Norwich before being replaced by second generation DMUs.

Some East Midlands Trains services stop at Attleborough in the morning and in the evening, but this is not one of them, as Class 158 Sprinter No. 158799 passes through Attleborough with a service for Liverpool Lime Street.

Abellio Greater Anglia Class 170 Turbostar No. 170205 sits at Attleborough with a service for Ely. Engineering works involving the construction of Cambridge North station meant that services were terminating in Ely.

In the remains of the summer sun, Abellio Greater Anglia Class 170 Turbostar No. 170204 sits at Thetford, awaiting departure for Cambridge.

Another test train, providing the same traction but in a different livery, comes in the form of Colas Rail Class 37 diesel locomotive No. 37116, which is seen passing through Thetford, bound for Cambridge via Great Yarmouth.

A new freight diagram that started on the Breckland Line was the regular Tunstead–Norwich Trowse aggregate service. The dark green of this Freightliner Class 66 No. 66604 makes a change from the normal sea of red seen on DB's Class 66s.

Nenta Railtours, based in North Walsham, regularly run railtours originating mainly from Norwich, but recent years have seen them starting from Great Yarmouth and Holt on the North Norfolk Railway. The tours are usually run with either a Class 47 or Class 57 diesel locomotive on either end with Mk 2 carriages in the middle. One such example is Class 47 No. 47854, which is seen passing through Thetford with an empty coaching stock (ECS) movement to Norwich, from where it will then form a railtour to Wales the next day.

Sometimes a two-carriage Class 170 Turbostar will deputise for a three-carriage Class 170 Turbostar. Here, No. 170271, devoid of most of its original Anglia Railways turquoise livery and the company logo on one carriage, arrives into Brandon with a service for Norwich. These units were built for Norwich–Cambridge services when the service was created in 2002, but were replaced in 2010 when they were found to be too small as passenger numbers increased.

Class 156 Sprinters sometimes deputise for Class 170 Turbostars, with one such example being seen here as Abellio Greater Anglia Class 156 Sprinter No. 156417 sits at Brandon, awaiting departure for Cambridge. At peak times, these units can become quite busy.

During the week, only one East Midlands Trains service stops at Brandon. This service arrives around 07.20, as seen here with No. 158864, which is awaiting departure for Norwich.

A long-running freight service that has been running down the Breckland Line for many years now is the Mountsorrel–Norwich Trowse aggregate service. In this image we see DB Class 66 No. 66148 heading through Brandon towards Mountsorrel.

When the Class 68s were in full swing down in East Anglia, they were regularly swapped so one or both could go back to Crewe, and sometimes Carlisle. Here is one example of a DRS Class 68 heading to Norwich to work the Short Set as No. 68017 heads through Shippea Hill.

DB Class 66 No. 66114 passes through Shippea Hill, heading back towards the Peak Forest. This freight train was late leaving Norwich and is hurrying to make up lost time.

Passengers can change at Ely for connecting services for Ipswich via Bury St Edmunds. Here, No. 170201 meets No. 170272, which awaits departure from Ely with an Ipswich service.

Ely station sees a lot of different varieties of freight, with all of them being hauled by Class 66 diesel locomotives. In April 2017, a pair of Colas Class 56 diesel locomotives, Nos 56078 and 56087, power through the station, bound for Harwich in Essex.

Sometimes steam engines will visit East Anglia, which gives a feel of yesteryear to the area. Britannia Class No. 70013 *Oliver Cromwell* departs Ely reception sidings running empty coaching stock down to Norwich in preparation for a tour the next day.

During Sundays in February 2016, the East Coast Main Line (ECML) was closed in the morning for engineering works. Because of this, some services formed of HSTs were diverted via Cambridge, Ely and March before re-joining the ECML at Peterborough. One such example is HST No 43058, which is seen passing through Ely with a service for Leeds.

Railtours are very common to East Anglia, with one of the main operators in the area being Nenta Railtours. All their railtours are diesel-operated, with Class 47s being preferred, as seen here at Ely as No. 47580 awaits time with a railtour for Carlisle.

The freight loop next to Platform 3 at Ely provides train enthusiasts with open views of freight trains that either stop or pass through Ely bound for either Felixstowe, Leeds, Birmingham or Crewe. Freight trains that are heading away from Felixstowe will be held in this loop awaiting a path onto the Peterborough line, as seen here with GBRf Class 66 diesel locomotive No. 66776 awaiting a path onto the Peterborough line at Ely with a freight service bound for Hams Hall freight terminal in Birmingham.

In August 2017 a freight train derailed between Ely and March, meaning that Arriva CrossCountry services were unable to go any further north, so instead they provided an Ely–Stansted Airport shuttle. Class 170 Turbostar No. 170110 was one of three Turbostars trapped south of Peterborough on the shuttle services. Here, it meets Abellio Greater Anglia Class 170 Turbostar No. 170204, which is bound for Cambridge.

The newest addition to the Breckland Line is Cambridge North, which opened in May 2017. Because of this station opening, Abellio Greater Anglia now extend their London Liverpool Street services to this station. Class 317 No. 317512 sits at Cambridge North with the slow service for London Liverpool Street.

Abellio Greater Anglia provide an hourly Norwich–Cambridge service, as seen here with Abellio Greater Anglia Class 170 Turbostar No. 170205 sitting at Cambridge North with a service for Norwich. At the time of writing, this was the last Abellio Greater Anglia Turbostar to be wearing the colours of the previous operator.

The bay platform at Cambridge North is shared between Abellio Greater Anglia and Great Northern for their services for London Liverpool Street and London King's Cross, as seen here with Great Northern Class 365 Networker No. 365512, which is awaiting time with a service for London King's Cross.

The yard next to Platforms 7 and 8 is normally the stabling point for many units that usually work London Liverpool Street services. One example is Abellio Greater Anglia Class 317 EMU No. 317503, which will remain in this yard until the morning peak on Monday, at which point most of the units in the yard will find themselves ferrying passengers between Cambridge and London.

The yard doesn't only host stabled units as seen in the image above, as the Network Rail Measurement Train (comprising an HST set) sometimes stops here. No. 43062 sits on the rear on the new Measurement Train, awaiting departure for Derby, where test trains such as these are usually based.

Freight isn't very common through Cambridge but one service that runs regularly is a freight service from Hoo Junction in Kent to Whitemoor Yard in March. This diagram has changed hands from DB Cargo to Colas Rail, who have a small fleet of Class 66 and Class 70 diesel locomotives for working this diagram. Class 70 No. 70810 passes through Cambridge, bound for Whitemoor with Freightliner Class 66 No. 66552 dead in tow.

For a long period of time, Class 365 Networker EMUs have provided an hourly service from London King's Cross to King's Lynn in Norfolk. These services usually leave London as an eight-carriage unit and then split at Cambridge, with the front four heading towards Ely, Downham Market and King's Lynn and the rear four carriages terminating at Cambridge, from where they lead the next service back to London King's Cross with the four-carriage unit that has come from King's Lynn. Here at Cambridge this procedure is taking place with No. 365515, which is awaiting departure for London King's Cross. Meanwhile, No. 365530 arrives into Cambridge with a terminating service from London King's Cross, which will later head to the yard.

Electrostars are a common sight at Cambridge with both Abellio Greater Anglia and Great Northern using them to commute passengers from Cambridge to London's King's Cross and Liverpool Street. Here, in Platforms 2 and 3, which are terminating platforms from London, Class 387 and Class 379 Electrostars Nos 387125 and 379006 are sitting at Cambridge, awaiting departure back to their various London termini.

Abellio Greater Anglia Class 170 Turbostar No. 170208 sits at Cambridge having completed the first diagram of the day. It will later head back to Norwich, stopping at nearly every station except for Cambridge North and Lakenheath.

The East Suffolk Lines

If Dr Beeching had gotten his way, the East Suffolk Line would have been destroyed and possibly turned into a road or a cycle path. Running on a 48-mile branch line, the East Suffolk Line connects the busy town of Ipswich with the seaside town of Lowestoft. The line opened in 1854 and consists of twelve stations, which are as follows:

- Ipswich
- Westerfield
- Woodbridge
- Melton
- Wickham Market
- Saxmundham
- Darsham
- Halesworth
- Brampton
- Beccles
- Oulton Broad South
- Lowestoft

The line has recently seen a lot of investment, with new track having been laid. This included a new passing loop at Beccles to allow a more frequent service to run on the line. Despite this, however, most of the East Suffolk Line is still single-track. There is an hourly service on the East Suffolk Line, which can see Class 153 Sprinters, Class 156 Sprinters and Class 170 Turbostars providing services up and down the line.

The East Suffolk Line now includes a 12-mile single-track branch line, which runs an hourly service from Ipswich to the coastal town of Felixstowe. This could easily be mistaken as a freight-only line due to the amount of freight trains that pass up and down the line with, at the time of writing, thirty-three freight trains traversing the line each day to multiple destinations across the UK and to other countries further afield. Despite this high level of freight that appears on this branch line, Abellio Greater Anglia are still able to provide an hourly service utilising a Class 153 Sprinter; however, sometimes circumstances mean that a Class 156 Sprinter or Class 170 Turbostar are used instead. The stations on the Felixstowe line are as follows:

- Ipswich
- Westerfield

- Derby Road
- Trimley
- Felixstowe

The Felixstowe Line, unlike many other freight lines in the UK, is un-electrified, which means that no electric freight locos can be seen on this line; instead, they start or finish at Ipswich before being uncoupled from their train, and a diesel locomotive such as a Class 66 or a Class 70 then finishes the last part of the journey.

The future looks bright for both of these lines though as a double-track extension has been approved for the Felixstowe line, meaning more freight trains can travel down the line without disrupting the hourly passenger service that currently runs. Moreover, when Abellio Greater Anglia acquired their new franchise, one of their commitments was that they are going to reintroduce direct services from London Liverpool Street to Lowestoft once their new stock has been built (the original service was cut in 2010 due to the stock being too small, meaning overcrowding was a regular occurrence).

Abellio Greater Anglia are also a member of the East Suffolk Lines Community Rail Partnership, which is a group dedicated to ensuring that a good train service is run on this line by allowing the local communities to have their say and provide ideas on how the service can be improved. A part of this is also allowing people to adopt railway stations to improve their appearance, which has become very evident with many stations along the East Suffolk Line looking very eye-catching.

Usually the unit provided for the hourly Felixstowe service is a Class 153 Sprinter DMU, but in some cases, such as if Ipswich Town football club are playing at home or if extra capacity is needed, then a Class 156 Sprinter or Class 170 Turbostar will step in and work the line all day. Here, Class 170 Turbostar No. 170273 departs Ipswich with a service for Felixstowe while Class 156 Sprinter No. 156418 awaits departure for Peterborough.

Services for Lowestoft can be served by any of Abellio Greater Anglia's DMU fleet. Here, Class 153 Sprinter No. 153335 sits at Ipswich with a Lowestoft service.

Abellio Greater Anglia Class 170 No. 170271 sits at Ipswich in the late afternoon sunshine with a service from Lowestoft; it soon departed back to the seaside town.

Abellio Greater Anglia Class 153 Sprinter No. 153314 arrives into Ipswich with a service from Felixstowe. These services do not spend very long sitting at Ipswich before turning around and departing again, with the service usually arriving at XX.54 and departing again at XX.58. The Class 153 usually provides enough capacity for this single-line branch.

The first station after Ipswich is Westerfield, where the Felixstowe Line diverges. All Felixstowe Line trains heading to the docks change lines, as seen with No. 66599.

All Felixstowe services stop at Westerfield. Here, No. 153306 picks up passengers bound for Felixstowe.

Services on the East Suffolk Line do not serve Westerfield in either direction. Here, Nos 170201, 156416 and 170203 pass straight through the station.

Freightliner Class 66 No. 66506 passes through, heading to Ipswich, which is where the locos are stabled when they aren't needed.

At the time of writing, the only part of the Felixstowe line that is double-track is at Derby Road. Freightliner Class 66 No. 66558 passes through while a GBRf Class 66 waits to restart its journey on the single-track section towards Westerfield.

The penultimate station on the Felixstowe Line heading towards Felixstowe is in the small village of Trimley in Suffolk. This station is small, with just one platform and no facilities, but despite this it is very popular with train enthusiasts for the very high amounts of liner freight going to and from Felixstowe Docks. Three freight operators can be seen passing through Felixstowe: DB Cargo Class 66 No. 66095, heading towards Peterborough with a driver's training run to Wakefield; GBRf Class 66 No. 66727 in its very distinctive Maritime livery, heading towards Peterborough after dropping off its liner train; and Freightliner Class 66 No. 66526, which is passing through Trimley on its way to Felixstowe with a liner train from Crewe.

Abellio Greater Anglia Class 170 Turbostar No. 170273 sits at Felixstowe.

On 22 July 2017, on a sweltering hot summer's day, Felixstowe was hosting a carnival in the street. Because of this, Abellio Greater Anglia provided a larger unit for the Felixstowe Line in the form of Class 156 Sprinter No. 156407. Here, it sits at Felixstowe, awaiting departure for Ipswich to pick up more carnival-goers.

Above and below: The final station on the East Suffolk Line is Woodbridge, which is served by an hourly service Mondays to Saturdays. Here we see Nos 156418 and No. 153335 awaiting departure for Ipswich.

Wickham Market, which serves the area of Campsea Ashe, is another station that sees an hourly service. No. 153335 arrives into the station with a service for Ipswich.

At Saxmundham the services meet, and here we see Nos 170271 and 153335 passing with their services for Ipswich and Lowestoft.

The basic yet very functional signal box at Saxmundham, once used for Radio Electronic Token Block on the East Suffolk Line, has now been upgraded to allow Track Circuit Block. This allows an hourly service to run on the line.

Abellio Greater Anglia Class 170 No. 170271 sits at Saxmundham, awaiting the signal to depart on the single-track section towards Wickham Market.

Above and below: Class 156 Sprinters Nos 156412 and 156418 depart and arrive into Saxmundham in the spring sunshine.

The small town of Halesworth, known for its malting, provides passengers with a connecting bus service to the coastal town of Southwold, which is very well known in the area for the Adnams brewery. This is another station that sees a regular service to both Ipswich and Lowestoft, with No. 170271 providing a service to the former.

At Beccles, the penultimate stop on the East Suffolk Line, the Ipswich and Lowestoft services meet before heading down their single-track sections. Here, Class 170 Turbostar No. 170273 and Class 156 Sprinter No. 156409 meet with services for Ipswich and Lowestoft respectively.

After arriving with a service for Norwich, No. 170272 waits to depart for Ipswich via the East Suffolk Line, where it will spend the rest of the day working.

A pair of sprinters can normally be seen here at Lowestoft as Nos 156409 and 156422 await departure for their destinations of Ipswich and Norwich.

The Great Eastern Main Line

The Great Eastern Main Line (GEML) is the main route from East Anglia to the capital as it runs from Norwich to London Liverpool Street through Norfolk, Suffolk and Essex. Passengers using the Great Eastern Main Line can reach the capital in roughly two hours, with Abellio Greater Anglia providing a half-hourly service on weekdays and Saturdays. The stations on the Great Eastern Main Line are as follows:

- Norwich*
- Diss*
- Stowmarket*
- Needham Market*
- Ipswich*
- Manningtree
- Colchester
- Marks Tey
- Kelvedon
- Witham
- Hatfield Peverel
- Chelmsford
- Ingatestone
- Shenfield
- Stratford
- London Liverpool Street

*These stations only are valid with an Anglia Day Ranger.

There are a further eleven stations between Shenfield and Stratford which make up part of the Metro services that run every fifteen minutes between Shenfield and London Liverpool Street, operated by TfL Rail.

The Great Eastern Main Line was opened in 1862 and has seen a variety of different traction providing the Norwich–London Liverpool Street services, with British Railways Standard Class 7 steam engines providing the traction before British Railways pulled the plug on steam-hauled services in the late sixties, later handing the reins over the Class 40 diesel locomotives, which were in turn replaced by the Class 47 diesel locomotives. With their maximum speed of 95 mph and their rapid acceleration, the Class 47s proved to be very popular.

The Great Eastern Main Line was electrified in the 1950s, but only as far as Colchester before it was fully electrified in the 1980s, with Ipswich in the early 1980s and the final part to Norwich in 1986. Since Norwich wasn't electrified, the Class 86 electric locomotives would operate the London to Ipswich section of the line before allowing the Class 47 to take over for the final part to Norwich. After 1986, the Class 86s completed the entire journey from Norwich to London Liverpool Street.

These Class 86s stayed on the Great Eastern Main Line into privatisation when Anglia Railways took over the line in 1997 from InterCity (a division of British Railways). This resulted in the stock of Class 86s, British Railways Mk 2 carriages and Driving Brake Standard Open (DBSO) being repainted from their recognisable InterCity livery into new, attractive Anglia Railways turquoise livery.

Towards the end of the Anglia Railways franchise, in 2004 the company started looking at the feasibility of replacing the elderly Class 86 locomotives with Class 90 locomotives, resulting in Freightliner Class 90s starting to appear on Norwich–London services. In 2004, Anglia Railways lost their franchise and National Express became the new owners of the Great Eastern Main Line, choosing the odd franchise name of ONE, which rather confused passengers. They replaced all the Class 86s, Mk 2 carriages and DBSOs with Class 90 electric locomotives, Mk 3 carriages and Driving Van Trailers (DVT), which made the services faster and meant they could hold more passengers.

In 2012, National Express lost their franchise to the current owners of the Great Eastern Main Line, Abellio Greater Anglia, who have kept the current stock running ten years after its introduction. However, the stock is due to be replaced in the future, with loco-hauled trains on the Great Eastern Main Line being replaced with EMUs after more than fifty years.

In the 1980s, an Anglia Day Ranger allowed passengers and train enthusiasts to travel to Colchester, but in recent years it has been scaled back to Ipswich, with additional tickets needing to be purchased before heading south towards Manningtree and Colchester. Despite this, passengers can still use an Anglia Day Ranger to get to and from Ipswich to locations such as Lowestoft via the East Suffolk Line and Ely/Cambridge via Bury St Edmunds.

As the night kicks in, No. 90005 awaits movement to Norwich Crown Point Depot. No. 90014 isn't finished with work yet as it awaits departure for London Liverpool Street one more time.

In 2016, while the home fleet of Class 90s were out for refurbishment, Abellio Greater Anglia hired in a Class 90 from DB. Here, No. 90034 sits at Norwich with a service for London Liverpool Street.

Abellio Greater Anglia Class 90 No. 90009 receives attention at Norwich before leaving for London again.

Services from Cambridge arrive into Norwich in time for a connection with the XX.00 service to London Liverpool Street. Here, No. 170207 arrives in time to meet No. 90008.

Norwich Yard is used by DRS to keep their diesel locos stabled until they are needed, as can be seen here with Class 37 No. 37425, Class 57 No. 57007 and Class 68 No. 68016.

In rare cases Class 321 electric multiple units will cover for an unavailable Class 90 set, which doesn't always prove popular due to the reduced seating and facilities. Here, No. 321358 sits at Norwich, awaiting departure for London Liverpool Street.

Abellio Greater Anglia Class DVT No. 82132 leads another train full of passengers into Norwich.

Abellio Greater Anglia Class 90 No. 90008 arrives into Diss on its first stop of many as it heads towards London Liverpool Street.

Diss is different to the other stations on the Great Eastern Main Line as there are no branch lines before or after the station. Because of this, Diss is only served by Class 90 sets to Norwich and London Liverpool Street every thirty minutes. Fresh from refurbishment, Abellio Greater Anglia Class 90 No. 90007 rests at Diss before departing for Norwich, where it will terminate.

No. 153306 rushes through Stowmarket as an ECS bound for the Sudbury line.

Freight is extremely common on the Great Eastern Main Line, with the main commodity being liner trains provided by DB, Freightliner and GB Railfreight. They all go to the Port of Felixstowe in Suffolk. The main operator is Freightliner, and here Class 66 No. 66587 is seen arriving into Stowmarket for a crew change before carrying on to Felixstowe.

Abellio Greater Anglia DVT No. 82152 speeds through Stowmarket with a service for Norwich.

Abellio Greater Anglia Class 170 No. 170273 sits at Stowmarket, picking up its last few passengers before the non-stop run to Ipswich.

All services to Cambridge and Peterborough from Ipswich are made up of Class 170 Turbostars, an example of which can be seen here as Abellio Greater Anglia Class 170 Turbostar No. 170206 sits at Stowmarket, awaiting departure for Cambridge.

Despite there being a half-hourly service to both Norwich and London Liverpool Street, every other service on the Great Eastern Main Line is faster. These services do not stop at Stowmarket, with the next station after Diss being Ipswich, followed by Colchester and then the service continues non-stop to London Liverpool Street. Here, No. 90015 speeds through Stowmarket on a fast service to London Liverpool Street.

Every autumn a seasonal freight train called the Railhead Treatment Train or RHTT for short comes to East Anglia. The train consists of two locos hauling sandite solution, which is sprayed onto the track to remove leaf mulch, which causes wheel slip and damage to train wheelsets. The RHTTs are based at Stowmarket and head towards Shenfield and Clacton before turning around and heading to Norwich via Bury St Edmunds, Ely and Thetford. In the image, DRS Class 57/3 No. 57306 leaves the passing loop at Stowmarket with a very early running RHTT service for Norwich. Note the muck on the side of the loco from RHTT duties.

It is not unusual to see a Class 156 Sprinter pass through Needham Market, as seen here with Abellio Greater Anglia Class 156 Sprinter No. 156409 passing through with a service for Ipswich.

Abellio Greater Anglia Class 170 No. 170202 sits at Needham Market station with a service for Bury St Edmunds.

Between Stowmarket and Ipswich lies the sleepy village station of Needham Market. This station has considerably lower passenger numbers compared to Stowmarket and Ipswich, the reason being that there are no services for London Liverpool Street or Norwich from this station. Instead, passengers would need to change at Stowmarket or Ipswich for a service to Norwich or London. Here, Abellio Greater Anglia Class 90 No. 90014 speeds through Needham Market with a service for London Liverpool Street.

An Abellio Greater Anglia Class 82 Driving Van Trailer (DVT) slowly passes through Needham Market with a service for Norwich. At the end of the platform is a temporary speed restriction of 50 mph, so trains not stopping here pass through slowly.

Abellio Greater Anglia Class 90 No. 90003 arrives into Ipswich with a service for London.

All services to Norwich and London Liverpool Street consist of a Class 90 electric locomotive, eight or nine Mk 3 carriages and a Class 82 Driving Van Trailer (DVT). They operate on a half-hourly frequency on weekdays and Saturdays, with an hourly service on Sundays. The DVT leads the train to Norwich, as seen in this image of Class 82 DVT No. 82107 arriving into Ipswich station.

The Norwich and London services usually meet at Ipswich as they arrive into the station within minutes of each other, as seen here with Abellio Greater Anglia Class 90s Nos 90015 and 90003 meeting with services for Norwich and London Liverpool Street.

Sometimes these Ipswich–London Liverpool Street services are made up of eight carriages, as seen here with two Class 321s, Nos 321310 and 321322, which are awaiting departure for London Liverpool Street from Ipswich. On this day, Ipswich Town football club had just finished playing and services were sitting at Ipswich station, waiting to ferry the supporters home.

There is an additional Ipswich–London Liverpool Street service that is usually operated by either a Class 321 or a Class 360 Desiro. These services are slower than the half-hourly services from Norwich as they stop at intermediate stations such as Marks Tey, Kelvedon and Witham. Abellio Greater Anglia Class 360 Desiro No. 360117 sits at Ipswich with a service for London Liverpool Street.

Normally the Norwich-bound Class 90 sets arrive into Platform 3 at Ipswich, but it isn't unusual to see a Class 90 set sitting in Platform 4. Here, Abellio Greater Anglia Class 90 No. 90009 is seen sitting in Platform 4 at Ipswich with a service for Norwich.

At the start of 2017, Abellio Greater Anglia announced that they would be sending off their Class 170 Turbostars for refurbishment, which included a complete interior refresh and a new livery. The first two-carriage Turbostar and the first three-carriage Turbostar to receive this treatment were Nos 170208 and 170270, as seen in this image at Ipswich. No. 170208 is awaiting departure for Cambridge while No. 170270 is awaiting attention from a fitter.

On 16 September 2017, Abellio Greater Anglia ran a railtour to raise money for a local charity called EACH. This railtour consisted of a DRS Class 68 diesel locomotive at either of a train that was made up of a complete Mk 3 rake and ran from Norwich to Ely and then back again, and up and down the Great Eastern Main Line. In the above image, DRS Class 68 No. 68001 passes through Ipswich with the second leg of the EACH tour towards London Liverpool Street.

Stock moves are a regular occurrence in East Anglia, with DRS sending locos and Mk 2 carriages back and forth and Abellio Greater Anglia moving their Class 90s and Mk 3 carriages for maintenance. Here, No. 57002 pops out of Ipswich Tunnel with a newly refurbished No. 90002 in tow, heading to Norwich.

Once an express service to London has left, a freight train soon follows. Here, No. 66955 is hot on the heels of No. 90003, which left ten minutes previously.

Above and below: Next to Ipswich station is the yard that Freightliner use to stable both their diesel and electric locomotives when they aren't needed, as seen here, with two examples being Nos 66503 and 70015.

Most liner trains come from the London direction, heading onto the Great Eastern Main Line at Stratford from the North London Line (NLL). One such example is Freightliner Class 66 No. 66558, sitting in the middle road at Ipswich, awaiting permission to enter East Suffolk Yard before heading onwards towards Felixstowe.

An old stalwart of the British railway network is the Class 86 electric loco. These locos have been working for well over fifty years and show no signs of giving up yet, despite their diminishing numbers. Freightliner are the only freight operator left using Class 86s, as seen here at Ipswich with Nos 86613 and 86622 in different Freightliner liveries as they arrive for a crew and loco change. The Felixstowe Line isn't electrified so a Class 66 or Class 70 diesel locomotive must take over on the final leg to Felixstowe.

The Ely–Ipswich Line (aka The Bury Line)

The Ely–Ipswich Line can be regularly overlooked but also plays a vital part in East Anglia as well as on an Anglia Day Ranger, and is known to many people as the Bury Line due to the medium-sized market town that is in the middle of this line. This line was built in 1846 and its stations are as follows:

- Ipswich*
- Stowmarket*
- Bury St Edmunds*
- Ely*
- March
- Manea
- Whittlesea
- Peterborough

- Ipswich
- Needham Market
- Stowmarket
- Elmswell
- Thurston
- Bury St Edmunds
- Kennett
- Newmarket
- Dullingham
- Cambridge

*These stations are only valid with an Anglia Day Ranger.

The main purpose of the Ely–Ipswich Line is to transport commuters from the busy town of Ipswich to the cities of Cambridge, Ely and Peterborough through two services, as seen above, both of which are operated by Abellio Greater Anglia. The two services are a twice-hourly Ipswich–Peterborough service and an hourly Ipswich–Cambridge service, and both are operated using Class 170 Turbostars, although Class 156 Sprinters can also be seen operating the line, deputising for an unavailable Class 170 Turbostar.

The Ely–Ipswich Line can also see a fair amount of freight operating over the line in the form of both aggregate traffic for Kennett, Barham (just outside Ipswich) and Bury St Edmunds and container trains for the Port of Felixstowe and for various places such as Doncaster, Leeds and Birmingham. The Kennett and Barham aggregate trains are only run by DB Cargo, whereas the Bury St Edmunds aggregate train is run by Freightliner. The container trains are operated by all the main freight operators in the UK, such as DB Cargo, Freightliner and GBRf. This freight flow can increase on weekends if the Great Eastern Main Line is closed for engineering works as they will come and go cross-country via Peterborough and Leicester to reach Ipswich and Felixstowe. Since the Ely–Ipswich Line is non-electrified, it means that all freight and passenger services on this line are diesel-operated only.

This line has also played an important role as a relief line. In the past, if there have been issues on the Great Eastern Main Line or the Breckland Line, passengers have been able to use the Ely–Ipswich Line to change at Stowmarket to reach Norwich, Ely or Cambridge. Though it increases journey times, it ensures that passengers are able to reach their destinations without having the need for a rail replacement bus or waiting for services to return to normal again.

The future looks good for the Ely–Ipswich Line as Network Rail and Abellio Greater Anglia are proposing increasing the single-track section between Ely and Soham to double-track, stopping the bottleneck that can occur if a passenger or freight service runs late, which holds up a service coming in the opposite direction. There is also the possibility of opening a new train station at Soham in Cambridgeshire, and Abellio Greater Anglia are proposing increasing the twice-hourly service from Ipswich to Peterborough to an hourly service when their new trains are built and delivered. Moreover, with Cambridge always expanding, it may not be long before another railway station could be proposed to serve a different part of this enterprising city.

Abellio Greater Anglia Class 170 Turbostar No. 170270 sits at Ipswich in the late February sunshine with a service for Peterborough.

Abellio Greater Anglia Class 156 Sprinter No. 156418 arrives into Stowmarket with a service for Ipswich.

Between Stowmarket and Bury St Edmunds lies the small village of Elmswell. The station here is unique because it is the only station within the boundaries of an Anglia Day Ranger that has travel agents on the platform.

Abellio Greater Anglia Class 170 Turbostar No. 170270 awaits departure from Elmswell with a service for Cambridge.

Freight is a regular occurrence on this line, but when the Great Eastern Main Line is closed this line sees an increase in container trains, as seen here with No. 66549 as it passes through Elmswell, bound for Crewe in the West Midlands.

Services from Peterborough don't stop at Elmswell, as seen here as No. 170273 powers through, heading towards Stowmarket.

Class 156 Sprinter No. 156412 slows to a stop at Elmswell with a service for Ipswich.

Services between Ipswich and Cambridge use three-carriage Turbostars, as seen here as No. 170201 awaits departure.

GBRf Class 66 No. 66753 passes through Thurston with a container train bound for Hams Hall in Birmingham.

Freightliner Class 66 No. 66548 powers through with a container train bound for Felixstowe.

Services from Ipswich heading towards Peterborough don't stop at Thurston either, and here No. 170273 passes through the station, heading towards its next stop at Bury St Edmunds.

GBRf Class 66 No. 66740 passes through with a container train bound for Felixstowe.

Every Saturday a light engine movement will run from Felixstowe to Peterborough, which is where Freightliner and GBRf are based in East Anglia. Seen here is No. 66759 as it heads to Peterborough non-stop.

Bury St Edmunds sees regular services serving the station, with both the Peterborough and Cambridge services stopping at Bury St Edmunds, as seen here as Abellio Greater Anglia Class 170 Turbostar No. 170273 arrives into Bury St Edmunds with the twice-hourly service for Peterborough.

In 2010 the services to Cambridge were improved from one to two carriages, which later became three when passenger numbers had increased to the point that a two-carriage train was too small. No. 170203 sits at Bury St Edmunds with a service for Cambridge.

Occasionally a Class 156 Sprinter will ply the line, as seen here as Abellio Greater Anglia Class 156 Sprinter No. 156422 sits at Bury St Edmunds with a late-running service for Cambridge.

A rarity was seen at Bury St Edmunds on 6 January 2018 when Abellio Greater Anglia Class 170 Turbostar No. 170202 sat at the station with a Peterborough service. Earlier in the week the middle carriage of this Turbostar had been removed as it was found to have a major fault that needed repairs. Instead of taking the entire unit out of service, it was simply shortened and sent back out into traffic.

A rather grubby No. 170270 sits at Bury St Edmunds, awaiting time with a service for Peterborough.

Just outside Bury St Edmunds is the small station of Kennett, which serves two villages nearby, called Kennett and Kentford, with the A14 dual carriageway being very audible in the background. Here, Class 66 No. 66951 passes through with a freight train for Felixstowe.

No. 170272 passes through Kennett, heading towards Peterborough. Like Elmswell and Thurston, the Peterborough services never stop here either.

Abellio Greater Anglia Class 170 No. 170270 pauses outside Kennett following a signal check before heading to Ipswich.

Abellio Greater Anglia Class 170 No. 170273 is making good time as it passes through, heading to Ipswich.

Abellio Greater Anglia Class 170 Turbostar No. 170201 arrives into Kennett with a service for Ipswich. Because of its location, this station is only served every two hours in each direction.

Abellio Greater Anglia Class 170 Turbostar No. 170201 arrives into Newmarket with a service for Cambridge.

Newmarket station, which is a shadow of its former self. When built, it had two platforms, waiting rooms and facilities, but now it only has one platform and no facilities. There is an hourly service to both Cambridge and Ipswich from Mondays to Saturdays and a service on Sundays every two hours.

Class 156 Sprinters can be seen deputising for a three-carriage Turbostar from time to time on Ipswich–Cambridge services, as seen here with No. 156416 sitting at Cambridge, awaiting departure for Ipswich.

In 2013, to promote more passengers to use the Breckland Line, Class 170 Turbostar No. 170208 was decorated in an attractive vinyl, showing all the different places that could be visited on that line. No. 170208, seen sitting at Ely with a service for Peterborough, shows off this vinyl.

Two-carriage Turbostars are a common sight on the Ipswich–Peterborough services, as seen here at Ely, as Class 170 Turbostar No. 170271 sits at Ely awaiting departure for Peterborough. Because of engineering works on the Bury St Edmunds line, this service started at Ely.

The Wherry Lines

The Wherry Lines are a collection of lines that are very popular with both train enthusiasts and holidaymakers alike every year and which run from Norwich along two lines to Great Yarmouth and along one line to Lowestoft.

The original line to Great Yarmouth, running via Reedham, was opened in 1844, with another line via Acle being opened in 1882. The line down to Lowestoft was opened in 1847.

The Wherry Lines are made up of fourteen stations altogether and the lines to Great Yarmouth are 18 miles via Acle and 20 miles long via Reedham, with the line to Lowestoft being slightly longer at 23 miles long. The stations are as follows:

- Norwich
- Brundall Gardens
- Brundall
- Lingwood
- Acle
- Great Yarmouth

- Norwich
- Brundall Gardens
- Brundall
- Buckenham
- Cantley
- Reedham
- Berney Arms
- Great Yarmouth

- Norwich
- Brundall Gardens
- Brundall
- Buckenham
- Cantley
- Reedham
- Haddiscoe
- Somerleyton
- Oulton Broad North
- Lowestoft

The Wherry Lines are usually served by Class 153 Sprinter DMUs, Class 156 Sprinter DMUs and Class 170 Turbostar DMUs, just like the Bittern Line, but there are two main differences. Firstly, the Wherry Lines see no freight services at all. Secondly, there is a loco-hauled service as well as the DMUs. Due to a shortage of units back in 2013, Abellio Greater Anglia created a new form of loco-hauled train known as the 'Short Set'. This was originally made up of two Class 47 diesel locomotives at either end with two British Rail Mk 3 coaches and a Class 82 Driving Van Trailer (DVT) sandwiched between them. This would run back and forth between Norwich, Great Yarmouth and Lowestoft and became very popular with train enthusiasts due to the diesel locomotives used and the popularity of loco-hauled trains over a diesel multiple unit.

On Summer Saturdays, which run from May to September every year, a Class 47 diesel locomotive used to drag a complete Class 90 set down to Great Yarmouth from Norwich to increase capacity on the line. This too was very popular with train enthusiasts as it again meant a loco-hauled train being dragged to the coast. Not only that, it was also very unusual to see a Class 90 electric locomotive on an unelectrified line with its pantograph down. Sadly, this was discontinued in 2014 after the continued unreliability of the Direct Rail Services Class 47s that were sent to East Anglia to run these services and the long process of having to set up the Class 90s in preparation for the London Liverpool Street leg of the journey.

Luckily, the 'Short Set' provides four Down and four return diagrams between Norwich and Great Yarmouth during Summer Saturdays between May and September, as well as the normal weekday services between Norwich, Great Yarmouth and Lowestoft. The latter, which is now made up of two Class 37 diesel locomotives at and three British Rail Mk 2 coaches, all of which are provided by Direct Rail Services, gives a nostalgic feel to this line. All Summer Saturday diagrams are non-stop between Norwich and Great Yarmouth to allow holidaymakers to reach these destinations quickly, and so train enthusiasts can hear the Class 37s powering away at full speed on the 75 mph line.

The Wherry Lines are a step back in time as the line from Brundall Gardens through to Great Yarmouth and Lowestoft is controlled by semaphore signals and manually controlled level crossings complete with signal boxes. There are also two swing bridges, which can be found at Reedham and Somerleyton on the Lowestoft line.

Sadly, at the time of writing Network Rail are in the process of upgrading the Wherry Lines, resulting in automatic level crossings and the removal of all the semaphore signalling and signal boxes, with the process due to be completed by spring 2019.

During February 2018, the Wherry Lines were closed for planned engineering works, which meant that no Short Set was needed. Here, DRS Class 37s No. 37423 and No. 37605 idle in Norwich Yard, waiting for their next duty.

Above and below: Abellio Greater Anglia Class 156 Sprinter No. 156409 sits at Norwich, awaiting departure for Cambridge while advertising 'Ride the Wherry Lines' on the bodyside.

Ride the Wherry Lines

wherrylines.org.uk

DRS Class 37 No. 37422 sits at Norwich, silhouetted in the early morning sunshine, with a service for Great Yarmouth.

Abellio Greater Anglia Class 156 Sprinter No. 156402 departs Brundall with a service for Norwich.

Abellio Greater Anglia Class 170 Turbostar No. 170202 arrives at Brundall with a service for Norwich.

Abellio Greater Anglia Class 153 Sprinter No. 153335 departs Brundall with a service for Great Yarmouth.

Class 153 Sprinter No. 153309 arrives into the small village of Lingwood with a service for Norwich.

A rarity in the form of Class 37 No. 37403 worked the Short Set on the Bank Holiday in May; here it arrives into Acle with a service for Norwich.

The Class 37 Short Set works from Monday to Friday, but not on weekends unless it is during the summer period or if Norwich City football club were playing at home. In these circumstances, Abellio Greater Anglia would use the Short Set to increase the number of seats available back to Great Yarmouth. 23 September 2017 was one of these days, as seen here with DRS Class 37 No. 37716, which sits at Great Yarmouth, awaiting departure for Norwich.

Recently refurbished Class 170 Turbostar No. 170208 sits at Great Yarmouth after arriving with a Summer Saturday non-stop service from Norwich. This will sit at Great Yarmouth for a brief amount of time before heading back to Norwich, again travelling non-stop via Reedham.

In 2016, Class 170 Turbostar No. 170204 suffered a major accident on the Breckland Line, which resulted in it being out of service for a long period of time. Because of this, Abellio Greater Anglia suffered more unit shortage issues and as a result they needed to make a deal with Direct Rail Services to hire a Class 68 Short Set as insurance. These three images show DRS Class 68 diesel locomotives No. 68018 departing Brundall with a service for Great Yarmouth, No. No. 68003 at Great Yarmouth awaiting departure with a service for Norwich and No. 68019 awaiting time at Lowestoft with a service for Norwich.

All of Abellio Greater Anglia's DMUs serve Great Yarmouth, as seen here with No. 153322, which is seen sitting at Great Yarmouth with a Norwich service, displaying the wrong destination.

Between Reedham and Brundall lies the quiet station of Cantley, which sees a regular service to Lowestoft and an occasional service for Great Yarmouth. This station boasts the last double semaphore signal in East Anglia, if not on the entire rail network. Here, Abellio Greater Anglia Class 170 Turbostar No. 170271 sits with a service for Lowestoft.

Most of the coastal services to Great Yarmouth and Lowestoft are served by Class 156 Sprinters and here is no exception as Abellio Greater Anglia Class 156 Sprinter No. 156418 arrives into Cantley with a service for Norwich.

The Ipswich and Norwich services usually meet at Lowestoft. Here, Nos 156407 and 37419 meet to allow passengers a connection to and from both Ipswich and Norwich.

A blast from the past can be seen outside Lowestoft station, as this sign, hailing from British Railways days, is still hanging. It also states that the station is called Lowestoft Central.

Acknowledgements

I would like to say thank you to the following people, who have helped make this book possible. To begin with I would like to thank my parents, for without their guidance and having them buy me my first camera I would have never found my love of photography – as well as their understanding as I dash in and out of the house at all hours of the day to get the pictures that make up this book. Secondly, I would like to thank all my train enthusiast friends, who have listened to me talk about trains (mainly the Class 170 Turbostar) many times and who have also accompanied me as I ventured around East Anglia. Thirdly, and not by any stretch of the imagination finally, I would like to thank the staff of Abellio Greater Anglia – the drivers, the guards and the platform staff, who with their friendly nature, their warm smiles and their great sense of humour have made travelling on the trains in East Anglia a great pleasure, which I hope will continue in the coming years. Thank you all for making this possible.

All images in this book are my own and were taken within the safety rules and regulations of the railways. Remember, the railways are a dangerous place and can kill if mistreated.